MW00744326

STRONG, CERTAIN AND ALONE

Poems in the voice of
Isaac Newton
1642 - 1727

ROSEMARY AUBERT

STRONG, CERTAIN AND ALONE

Poems in the voice of Isaac Newton, 1642 - 1727

Rosemary Aubert

ISBN: 978-1-77242-097-5

Carrick Publishing

Cover Art and Design Sara Carrick

Dedication:

This book is respectfully dedicated to the memory of Stephen Hawking.

Collected Poems

Two Kinds of Honey
Picking Wild Raspberries
Lenin for Lovers
Rough Wilderness
Strong, Certain and Alone

Foreword:

These poems were generated by my experience of seeing objects that belonged to Newton during visits to his haunts at Cambridge as well as long periods of personal study of his work and his enormous influence on the worlds of science, philosophy and dedicated intellectual endeavour.

Rosemary Aubert, 2018

Contents:

GRAVITY

Pull of the apple, the earth and the moon.

Invisible material desire, which like all desire

shades within the piercing ray of repulsion.

Pull of the sun and pull away.

Pull of my mother's arms—then push and push.

Pull of night, of day, of days…

I feel my own good feet fight the stony ground that bred
me.

Beneath, the bones of my father soldered to his grave.

What is this? Who knows or will know or cares?

No one.

Though the feet of no one, like mine

are bolted by some kind of love

to the skin of the spinning world.

LIGHT

Newton temporarily deforms his eyeball by pressing the back of it with a needle

Is light a miracle?
Or is it some mundane thing?
This everywhere fire of bright abundance
this soft gem in the black crown of night.

Is light a star as a star is light?
Is it my name writ high before I had
the wit to read it? Or after all?

What is light?
Is it an object?
Is it a being?
Does it inhabit my prism
the way a felon inhabits his cell?

I ask again as I have thus far always asked:
What is light?
Is it a miracle?

If I take this needle
and stick it into
the dark back of the seeing orb,
will I learn light?
Or will I kill it?

Here now—
let us see.

GETTING RID OF ME

They said I was born the size of a quartpot
that my large head
held up by a bolster around my neck
swayed sometimes on its stalk
as if it were already weighted
by an anchor in the sea of dreams.

My good father was claimed
by the God who had made him
before I arrived.
I basked in the brightness of my mother
until she, too, fled
making her home in the home of another
who deemed my disposal
a condition of their union.

So I have always been alone.
No voice in my head other than mine own.
No pressure of someone else's skin against my skin.
No eyes seeking mine, wanting answers, wanting in.

I have heard it said
that a man without a wife
is half dead
has only half a life.

If so
I've had the half I craved—
the sweet empty space
the wide clean plane
the silence at the heart of time.

Mine.

They thought, when they got rid of me
that I might mourn and seek.

Instead, I sing
and sing again to know
that no one hears
or mars my tune
with the damning judgement
of the ear.

THE SCHOLAR

Cambridge University 1661

I came to its white towers,
green fields beyond the river Cam.
The small sharp stones of its myriad paths
pierced the soles of my country boots.

I came to its pillared arcades
its shadowed, secret squares
where the statues of scholars past
glared down on me as if to say:
"Go home and mind your sheep."

I knelt in pilgrim-polished pews
where the ghost of great Erasmus lingered
and prayed in the nave of Christ Church
whose marble pinacles teased the sky
then soared toward heaven and the one true God.

I came a *tabla rasa*, an unscratched slate
an unlicked cub, a farmer's son
taught by the sun and the moon,
the shadows of seasons,
the apple's fall.
Student of light
and the angle of the stars.

I saw at once what I needed:
the scholar's garb
a decent wig
a strong-nibbed pen
several small notebooks
and a mind determined to know
every knowable thing.

STOURBRIDGE 1

The Fair is founded for the sake of the Leper Chapel at Cambridge

That they might pray,
their knarled hands lifted
above the sickness and the fear,
to the God who made them
and unmade them
as He saw fit;

that they might come
to a place in which
they'd find no others,
a place of white peace
and the shriven light of clerestory windows;

that they might know
that their ravaged faces,
shorn of features,
robbed of any claim
to human form,
might here shame no one
and be as the faces of angels;

I, John, King of England
grant this Fair
so that whatever will be built here
shall be maintained
and be for all time hence
as a shrine to the sorrow of lost bodies
and the glory of sanctified souls.

STOURBRIDGE 2

Entertainers at the Fair, a pantoum

The minstrels strummed and blew and smacked the taut-
    skin drum
and giants danced among the dwarves
like stars around the moon.
A conjuror tricked a golden coin from out the ear of a
    yearling child

And giants danced among the dwarves
spun like tops and laughing fell.
A conjuror tricked a golden coin from out the ear of a
    yearling child.
A learned pig snorked answers to a sum,

spun like a top and laughing fell
among the farmers and their well-fed wives.
A learned pig snorked answers to a sum
though wise men scoffed and fools turned away.

Among the farmers and their well-fed wives
like stars around the moon
though wise men scoffed and fools turned away
the minstrels strummed and blew and smacked the taut-
    skin drum.

FOR SALE AT THE FAIR

At each September, these things gather themselves:
Fish from the yielding river or stolen from the sea.
Tar from the grimy pits where black-stained men sweat
   in the yellow light.
Wool the dumb sheep give
so that the wordy parson may have his woolen shawl.
Books from the libraries of wealthy men or written in
   the scholar's hand
books and the oil to read them by.
Cabinets and tables and bedsteads and desks—
gift of the turner's lathe, the joiner's deft fit.
Nails and hinges and catches and pulls.
Cotton from over the ocean and flax from the
   neighboring hills.
Pewter, silver, copper, gold.
Tobacco and pipes, bowls and plates.
Soap and perfume and powder to whiten the faces of
   ladies and beaus.
White, they'll be, white as the moon,
which rises over all
and turns the Fair into night dance
where
the minstrels strum and blow and smack the taut-skin
   drum.

BUYING THE PRISM AT THE STOURBRIDGE FAIR

Seduction is gravity
the pull of sweet promise.
Revelation is sweet promise.
I will tell you.
I will show you.
What I am will be set before you
touch and taste.
Temptation
    Have me and you have all.
    Have me and you shall be
    all
    you long to be.
Carry me.
Carry me to you.
Carry me with you.
And you will learn
that light is life
that light is what you came for.
That light is what you are.

THE PLAGUE 1665-1666

Men who would be spared, fled
until the empty streets were filled with wolves
who finding nothing left to eat
sank back into the fetid wood
and ate the ones who hid there.

Men who stayed in town perished too.
No quarantine secure enough.
No lock sufficient.
No lie.
No pretence.
No escape
from the warden, the wagon, the pit.

I could write of the agony:
the dagger in the skull
the devil's dark kisses: buboes and rash.
Breath sealed forever in the lungs.

The doors of Cambridge slammed me out.
I went to an old pure place
and there among the fields, I staked my claim.
So write instead of my haven
Among the clean and cleansing stars.

THE BAD SHEPHERD

October 28, 1659

I have been called here to admit
and do so admit
before this, the manor court of Colsterworth,
that I, first-born of Hannah Ayscought Newton Smith,
Isaac, to wit,
did suffer the sheep of my mother
to break the stubbs of 23 furlongs of fence
and did allow those sheep
to wander without halt
and thence to trample our neighbor's field
ruining his corn, his livelihood and his day.

And further, I confess
that I did willfully subvert
the servant of our house
sent to instruct me
in the proper art of watching sheep
and did purposefully bribe him
to do *my* work
while I repaired to the library of Joseph Clark
and there devoured my hours
reading books.

I was, sirs, minding a different fold
wherein I saw numbers flee
from the fenced-in fields
of earth-bound Euclid
following Descartes into the immeasurable ether.

The sheep asked to be freed, sirs
as I ask you now.

Let me be.
Let me roam.
Where few can follow
and none confine.

AT CAMBRIDGE

"Truth is the offspring of silence and unbroken meditation." IN

I don't need love
the sanctuary of the weak.
I don't need society
with its wanton disregard
of stillness and calm.
I don't need wine.
I don't need rich food.
I don't need sleep
until it comes of its own accord.
I don't need friends.
I don't need music
or dancing
or leaping about like a fool.
I don't need gaming
or hunting.
I don't need travel
except the travel of the mind
between truth and the proof of truth.
I don't need idle conversation
the meaningless morning hello
the feeble goodnight at the
predictable arrival of dark.
I don't need pets.
I don't need holidays.
I don't need family.

I don't need love.
I need to be alone.
I need to think.
I need to see
with my eyes hard shut.
I need to hear
the sound of my own heart
beating in my ear.

RED I

Red
of blood
of fire
of the nascent
and dying sun
of mercury
of Mars.

Red
of fury
of danger
of longing
of cessation
of warning
of war
of victory
of the soldier drowning
in the swift discharge
of his arteries.

Red
of majesty
of martyrs
of celebrants
and kings
of emperors
of cardinals
of the robes of the Lord.

Red
of roses
of poppies
of the robin's belly
and the little crimson flowers
that blow
beneath my feet.

Red
of a rich spice sauce
of pomegranates
of strawberries
of tomatoes
and cherries
and plums.

Red
of the apple
that fell from the tree
and made me.

RED II

Cochineal

Imagine the reddest red you can.
Try piercing yourself
and watching your blood spurt
burble up
from the wound of your wondering.

Imagine Mary Queen of Scots
kneeling at the guillotine
in her special shirt.
Red of rebellion.
Red of saturation.

Imagine the martyrs of cinnabar
who perished for the richness
of a lady's gown
of a cardinal's cloak.
Cinnabar, vermillion, ore of mercury.
Mine this, prisoner. Mine this, slave.
And die for your sins and your servitude.

Imagine red ochre
from French cliffs
ochre tinted with hematite—
choice of artists who had no choice:
painters of the prehistoric caves.

Imagine madder root
and dragon's blood—
sap of *Croton, Calamus, rotang,*
varnish of Italian violins.

Imagine brazilwood
powder of red wood
namer of nation.

Imagine
that creatures
including ourselves
see red to keep us
from eating unripe fruit.

Imagine all this.

Then imagine the cactus deserts
of the New World.
Imagine prickly pear
and a small brown bead
a pellet, a pebble, a nut
feeding on the dusty cactus.

Imagine this insect
this bug
this cochineal.

Imagine killing it
and releasing with the press of your thumb
a red to defy red
to define red
to distill a red so pure
it vanquishes all other notions of red.

And then imagine how many billions died
and die still and will die
their blood staining the flags
of galleons
racing across the red-hungry sea.

RED III

My Favourite

After I died
someone made an inventory
of my goods.

I had crimson window dressings
a crimson bed with crimson drapes
crimson wall hangings
a settee with a bright crimson cushion.

I had a crimson chair
designed for my leisure
and six crimson pillows
to ease my back
with down.

I had many other things
as befits a man of science
a friend of the court
a dignitary of the realm.

But I liked my red things best.
Why?
Because I liked my red things best.

Based on "A true and perfect inventory of…Sir Isaac Newton. 5 May, 1727. By Virtue of Commission of Appraisement, Court of Canterbury."

ALCHEMY I

Prisca Sapentia

Pristine wisdom made molten
and mixed with the secrets
of fire and time.

What the ancients knew:
that nature is
the clear, strong voice of God.
That all things
are the same thing:
creation the face of Creator.

Here's what I do
to seek the magic stone
to distill the elixir of life
to find what the ancients found
to quaff the cup of their knowing:

In secret
at night
when no other man sees me
nor hears the cackle
of my black fire
nor breathes the air of my chamber
(once foul, now scented as of lily and of rose)
I take shavings of iron

child of anvil, file and flame
and I take the body of an orange
the skin, the pulp, the juice
the innocent acid of the docile south—
and I take mercury
teardrop of the pulsing moon
milk of the silver cow
slithersnake among the speckled rocks
metal music—

I take these three
and wed them
and wait
until the elders in their graves
whisper to me
and tell me how long to tarry
by the crucible and the cauldron
and what to pray to the stars for
and what to hope.

ALCHEMY II

The Star Regulus of Antimony

I have spent these many hours
calling down the spirits
of this place
reaching to touch
bodies
that other men
cannot and would not see.

I have spent these many hours
purifying my spirit
knowing that the high price
cannot be won
by a low man.

I have spent whatever remained of my youth
in search of the star crystal
the "little king"
the regulus of antimony.

This element, this atom
was supposed to be
a key
a magnet
the changer
the allower
of all magic.

Instead
I find the old earth
the aged metals
gold, silver, iron, tin, mercury, lead, copper
that have not changed
and will not change.

Now I am told
by all I touch and smell and see
that *I* am the magnet
that I must draw down
by my own and only power
all that can be learned
of earth and its ways.

The star regulus of antimony
shines in the darkness
and shows no other truth than this:
I only
am the star
and the element
and the eye.

BEING A SIZAR AT CAMBRIDGE

At the Great Gate of Trinity
on the day I arrived
I encountered the statue
of Henry the Eighth.

I thought not then
as I think not now
of any wife
or of any woman
except Hannah, my mother
who, though rich,
rendered me poor enough
to have to
bow and shuffle
and run
at the beckoning
of men younger
and otherwise lesser
than myself.

Boys these bosses were—city boys
with contempt
for a man from the farms
and the sleepy vales of dumb sheep.

I woke these students each dawn
rousing them from their easy slumber
fearsomely truncating my own.

I polished the boots
they left lined by their doors.
I dragged their sodden linens
down long corridors
to filthy laundry carts.

I brought them beer
and buns
and bacon and beef
gifts of the docile herds
that grazed the emerald banks
of the Cam.

I lowered my head
when I met them
in Trinity's stone colonnades.
I bore their insults—
the way they shouted—"Hey…"
and teasing tempted me into
their arguments, their politics, their foul jokes
that I almost never understood.

I suffered these things deeply
but not for long.
Soon it was I
who ordered the saplings about.

Bring me my bow of burning gold.
Bring me water, my bread.
Bring me my meat, my wine.

And when you come
note that the statue you pass
in the courtyard
is a statue of me.

MONEY LENDER

This is a small thing.
Not usury as some would have it
but a just return on an enabling debt.

A matter like kindness
or sharing
or provision: I help you.
And when the time comes
you help me, too.

Risk is a multiplicand.
Something multiplied
or multiplying something else.

So I lend you this pound
and by a little gift of time
you give it back
and it has become
more than it had been.

The universe has
many ways of always
staying the same.
This is not one of them.

INFINITY AND THE CALCULUS

Consider the tortoise and swift-footed Achilles.
No matter how slowly the tortoise crawled
no matter how quickly Achilles covered
half the turtle's distance
he could never catch up.

Infinity is like that.
One, plus half of one, plus half of the half...
Add all these to reach two someday.

Or never.

I needed infinity.
At first, I thought
to square the circle
as others had "squared" it before me.

But then I saw so much more:
a curve
like the curve a planet makes
as it soars around the sun.
A curve beneath which lies
an infinity of minute rectangles
and a way to reckon the sum of them.

And I saw also
an infinity of points
on the slope of the curve.

I called these things
"fluents" and "fluxions".
Points become lines.
Lines become planes.

I saw an infinity of instants
in any motion
an infinity of motions
in any change.

And I knew
I'd found a way
to hold the world still
as if the thumb of the Maker
could come down
hard upon it.

GOD IN GRAVITY

By Isaac Newton and Isaac Watts

Every particle of matter attracts every other particle with
    a force proportional to the product of the masses
    and inversely proportional to the square of the
    distance between them.

I sing the mighty pow'r of God, that made the
    mountains rise,
That spread the flowing seas abroad, and built the lofty
    skies.
I sing the wisdom that ordained the sun to rule the day;
The moon shines full at His command, and all the stars
    obey.

The ancients worshipped the plodding stars
measured their slow steps
across the black sky
watched for the return of the hunter
when autumn came
with arrows in his dazzling quiver.
Who is this hunter
Who flees from the King of Day?
And who are his companions
who come time and again
crowding the night with their light?
Numbers.

Equations.
Naught but measurable things.
The full heavens
balancing each planet
against its other and opposite self.

I sing the goodness of the Lord, who filled the earth
    with food,
Who formed the creatures through the Word, and then
    pronounced them good.
Lord, how Thy wonders are displayed, where'er I turn
    my eye,
If I survey the ground I tread, or gaze upon the sky.

There has to be a way
of tossing anything out:
an apple, a star, myself.
And watching it speed
hot back toward another thing.
A way without spirit or ether.
Without destiny or design.
Simply the desire
of all things in this world
for all other things.
I want God out of gravity.
I want no mystery, no ministry.
I want the force that harnesses everything
to harness me to truth.

Matter not myth.
Material not miracle.
My own body
scion of the wild sea
and drawn inexorably toward it.

There's not a plant or flower below, but makes Thy
 glories known,
And clouds arise, and tempests blow, by order from Thy
 throne;
While all that borrows life from Thee is ever in Thy care;
And everywhere that we can be, Thou God, art present
 there.

I want to throw away
magic
mystery
majesty
grace
and all but the ground I stand on.
But I can't.
I want not to be drawn.
But I am.

HOW TO CAPTURE A RAINBOW

"This Bow never appears, but where it rains in the Sun-shine, and may be made artificially by spouting up Water which may break aloft, and scatter into Drops, and fall down like Rain."

Isaac Newton *Optics*

Red
Orange
Yellow
Green
Blue
Indigo
Violet

Direct into your eager eye
the splintered spectrum of the sun.
White light made of all light
breaks and becomes
the heavenly lamps of each:

Red blood of soldiers.
Orange of the sky in an hour with no name.
Yellow of the sweet bird's wing.
Green of the sea and the summer fields.
Blue of the eyes of babes.
Indigo of the veins in an old man's hand.
Violet of night light.
And then nothing and absence and dark.

Here's how you capture a rainbow:
Fling water into the sun.
Or run
when you see a certain dark cloud
and opposite
the bright, belligerent rays refusing
to be rendered obscure.

The sky gives rainbows
and the snow
and a certain cut of glass
and a small hole
in a piece of black board
fastened to my window
and directing into my eager eye
the splintered spectrum of the sun.

THE PROFESSOR

You look out and see
nobody looking back.
It's a relief really.
And you conduct the whole lecture
in your head.
Puts your mind at ease.
Not to mention your mouth.

Sometimes—though rarely—
you see a pair of bead-like eyes
trained upon you
like the twin barrels of a farmer's gun
aimed at the wolf among the sheep.

And then you roar
to send them off
with fine stories of
how crazy you are.

I'm not a teacher.
Nor ever have been.
What's in my head
is mine.

I have spent long hours
trying to convince
people of that fact.

If I see the high white moon
perform a trick of gravity
among the reaching waves
or skitter around the steadfast sun,
it is mine.

I am not a writer
a reporter
an artist
nor a gravity-dancer myself.
I am I
and all I see
and think
and figure
and frame
is me, too.
And no one else or else's.

I HATE TO TAKE A BATH

I hate to take a bath
because I know what lives in the water
because I know what lives on my skin
and that it has
a reason to live there.

I hate to take a bath
because I don't want to remove my boots
that have grown so sweetly accustomed
to my feet.

I hate to take a bath,
to see my emptied clothes
balanced on the back
of a chair
already precarious
from the weight of books.

I hate to take a bath
in case someone comes
and finds me as God made me
(though no one ever does).

But most I hate to take a bath
because what starts warm
or even hot
relinquishes energy and
passes to another state
by the icy time I remember
where I am
and have the wherewithal
to abandon some exquisite thought
that's kept me there—
a captive of the bucket and the brush—
until day has turned to night
and the woman I was supposed to summon
to bring towels and soap and such
has long since gone home
to the dry embrace of her own.

LOSING MY TEMPER

There is no warning
no signal passed
from one sentry to another
no sentry
only the clenched power of fury
a tiny key to turn
in the giant door of rage.

When it comes
it is the seventh wave
the big one
the one that
savages the strand
and casts the creatures of the sea
high upon the waterless sand.

Rage akin to killing.
Anger as murderous
as the thief in the night
who takes everything:
chattels, light and life.

I don't want this
but it wants me
and when it comes
I go wherever it leads.

I would smash my crucibles.
I would rip my books until
the tattered pages
swung upon the spine.
I would tear red cushions
into a cyclone of feathers
and shred the crimson curtains
of my bed.
I would take my enemy's stupid head
between my fingers
and squeeze until
his words had no way
to exit from his throat.

I do none of this, of course.
I am a civil man and a servant of God.
And I value the peace and unity
of His world.

But sometimes
I feel the boiling blood
rush from my heart
into my hands.

And then...

FATIO: FORCE ACTING AT A DISTANCE

I was reading in the Common
when I looked up and noticed you.
By then, how many students had I had?
Dozens, hundreds, a thousand?
An infinity passing before my eyes
like clouds
or the birds that skitter from
tower to tower
their chittering making a mockery
of the staid, still silence of Trinity
and in all that time
I never noticed one of them
sufficiently to distinguish
him from any other.

But you—
I can't say now what I noticed first
because I have only thought of you
as beautiful
from that moment.
Your slender body,
your face bright with knowledge
and the search for it
and some other look
that I know now—but not then.

I raised my eyes from my book
and saw you
and saw nothing else
for a good long time.

Here is force acting at a distance:
the cold stone moon
not once, not ever moved to anything
anyone would call love.
The sun burning with inextinguishable fire--
the reaching flame, the heat.

Force acting at a distance.
Had I been blind
I would have felt
the power of you walking through
the gate of Trinity,
the gate of my ancient virgin life.
Had I been deaf
I would have heard
the bell toll
the hour of my first falling,
falling into you.

As the moon falls toward the sun
until it is pushed away
by a power both frightening and benign.

I might have been consumed.
Instead I was inflamed.
And feel that first momentous heat
still and always.

As I imagine the marble moon feels
when the fire of light falls upon it
illuminates in the black of night:
desire.
Force of attraction
at such a distance
or no distance
between my mouth
and the width
of your sweet lips.

WHAT THE SHADOWS SAY

A man needs no timepiece, no calendar
when he can read
what the shadows say.

When I was a child
I built a sundial
in my grandmother's garden.
She regularly dismantled it
not wanting stones among the lillies.

So I built a clock out of leaves
and branches
and soon saw
how time seemed to change
with the seasons.

In our fields
I told time by
the shadows of our sheep.
Best I loved noon in
the summer
when the dumb things stood
hot and still and stupid
and made almost no shade at all.
I took a stick and shook it
and watched them run
barely darkening the grass
beneath their feet.

Later I learned
how to draw the analemma
how it takes the whole year
to do it
to make a chart of the sun's path
by plotting the shadow
of a peg on the windowsill
against the unmoving wall.
It's like 8-shaped infinity
that shadow
and where it stops
is always where it starts.

So a man who reads shadows
needs no calendar, no clock,
though the hours, the days
pass from him, too
and the final shadows wait for him
and the sun spins away
and its patterns mark
the place of his grave.

LAUGHTER

"During five years, Humphrey saw Newton laugh only
    once." Richard S. Westfall

I don't laugh.
Why should I?
To laugh when alone
is the signature of madness.
To laugh with another
is to acknowledge
a mutual weakness.
And anyway
what is funny?
The perfection of God's world?
The secrets that bind me
to hours of dark labour?
The passing of time?
The clever moon
in its many guises?
The spin of the earth
toward and away—
night and day…

What is worthy
of a wise man's laugh?
Only himself
and I will not stand
for that.

THE CANDLE AND THE BOOK

I had a book I worked on
for twenty years—
a book of colours.
Many the long day
I laboured on it
watching as the beams of the sun
split and split again
as I sat by the window
thinking hour after hour
about how they managed that
and why.

I did, as I always do
hundreds of experiments,
changing sometimes
only a millimetre
only a second.
I recorded these things
with a precision unlike
any I'd achieved before
until I had
tables and charts and
proof beyond proof
of the truths my testing
showed me.

At night
when only the moon lit the sky
when only the weak stars
spared their puny light,
I used a candle
to allow my labours
to flame away
the countless hours of dark striving.

I did not know
though I should have
who the enemy was
and how strong
and how patient
waiting for me
to go away
which one day,
I did.

And then it struck
and it took in a moment
all the twenty years
of watching and writing,
all the mornings
spent by the window
all the sleepless nights
of learning the code of colour
of writing its secrets down.

A candle took that book
and from the ash of its pages
arose
nothing.

It was gone that morning.
It is gone now.

And never again
shall I touch those pages
nor remember
nor discover again
what the fire took,
its bright light breaking
into colour after colour after colour.

EVERYTHING

What I wanted
was to explain everything.

I could feel
as I stood solid
on the still earth
all the planets pulling
and my mind was pulled
as though I were a planet
and the sun grabbing me
before, in indifference
it flung me away.

On the pebbled beach
the trembling waves
were my fingers
fingers
of salt
of ice
of sand
of time
fingers crushing
rock into
tears of stone.

At night I watched
millions of stars
or none
never knowing
never proving
that they were really there.

I caught the wind
in my hair and my eyes and my clothes
breath of the whirling globe—
unless it were a windless day
on which I felt
earth hold its breath.

I saw nature as a kingdom
as the court of the one true Monarch
and never did I question
the Creator of the comets
soaring from the farthest reaches
of the perfect dark.

I see sometimes the print
of one of my fingertips on some soft thing.
I suspect this is my mark.

I have seen such a print
made by the Master of all.

It is all.

THE MADNESS OF A SLEEPLESS MAN

It is always as though
I am the only one.

Around me I sense
the birds in their black nests—
the trees of night sheltering them
from any opening of eye
or shift of feather
or beat of a folded wing.

I sense the dozing peasants
in their soft hovels
cast along the borders of our fields
slumbering as seeds slumber
with no fearsome thought
of morning or of spring.

On the pond I hear
the rhythm of the hearts of swans
slowed to the pulse of the waveless water
that only now and then
laps against the grass.

Lying awake hour after hour
I hear the stars

flash and sizzle and clap hard
against each other.
But then, I always hear *that*.
So it counts as silence
to my accustomed ear.

What I'm saying is
a man who cannot sleep
hears every little thing,
even his own breath
struggling in his dreamless lungs.

Until—eyes wide with the fatigue
of watching nothing,
he hears finally
the college clock striking morning.

And then begins
the sleep-dozed day
and the voices of men
he does not know
calling his name
and numbers dancing
as though they knew a gavotte.
And the boy at the door
who brings the bread
becoming suddenly ten boys
hopping about as though it were he
and not myself
who is mad.

THE MONSTER OF THE MINT

This is the name they gave me
and this I proudly was.

Half the reprobates were chipping coins
grinding away
until one shilling
magically became two leaner ones
by the forging of the filings of the first
into a second.

The other lot—
more dexterous, clever and well-supplied
were counterfeiters
making pounds by the batch
as though they were biscuits
or scones for their tea.

I pursued them without cease.
I sent my faithful stalwarts
by horse, by coach, on foot
to a dozen counties.
I went myself
in cloak and hat drawn low and mask.

I found them
nabbed them
yanked them through the courts
until came the day on which
they all lay dead at the gibbet's foot.
Hanged, quartered, drawn and done
just as they deserved.

I persisted
until the King's round coins
knew no diminishing.
Until a pound became again
a real pound
and a shilling pulled down the pocket
the way the earth pulls down the moon.

THE FIRE AT THE CENTRE OF THE TEMPLE

"The fire shall ever be burning upon the altar; it shall never go out. (Leviticus 6:13)

Everyone knew in the days of Solomon the Wise
that the fire at the centre of the Temple
was lit by the hand of God,

that the Holy of Holies was guarded
by the outstretched wings of cherubim
clothed in gold, scented by wood
hewn from the Cedars of Lebanon.

They did not then know
that the centre of our universe is the sun
or they would have seen
that the fire at the centre
is the giver of life.

I studied Hebrew
so that I might know
how the Temple was perfectly formed.

I study the universe
so that I might know
that the sun that gives us life
was lit by the hand of God.

GETTING RID OF FATIO

I trusted you.
I told you secrets
not only of my work
but of myself,
secrets you laughed at
and which, at first,
I dared to laugh at, too.

More,
I told you the secrets of my life,
of the place that I came from
the people—
I trusted them, too
until they sent me away
with nobody's regret but my own.

I let you be with me
in the hours no other could share,
granting the treasures of darkness.
I convinced myself I was keeping
the best part of night for us
and always would.
A fool thinks
his dreams are his to control.

Now you say
you're done with me.

Fine.
Take whatever you came with:
your ideas
your understanding
your puppy enthusiasm
for all that was new
or seemed new
because you saw it
through a wise man's eyes.

Take whatever you came with:
your lithe limbs, your fine head
bent in the light from our window
to study what I showed you:
that white light lies
bearing rich secrets that can be broken
by a shard of glass.
The treasures of light.

You thought I gave you all I had
and so are done with me.

But I kept for my own, these tears.
Before you, before now
I thought them locked forever
by my faithless mother
a long time ago.

So go.

I know I will never see you again.
Forgiveness?
I think not.

I write in haste.
I see a great black shadow
out of the corner of my eye.

You are there.
You are gone.
Fine.

But still,
I shall be mad without you.
I shall be mad.

BALANCING ON THE EDGE OF BREAKDOWN

I am an icicle.
Do you know that thing?
You can hold water in your hand.
You can pierce your hand
with water
and watch your own blood freeze.

Blood freezes in my veins
when I remember
there is no hope.

Some bastards think
the world is constructed
like a clock.
Ticking idiots.
A great big clock.
Do you know that thing?

A great big clock.
Some nights time cries
in the darkness,
flies across the fields
of Cambridge,
kisses the sheep
asleep in the Cam.

No, you dimwit!
The Cam is a river—
not a field.
The white numbers form a field
on which the axes dance.
What does that mean?

By the rivers of Babylon—
Babble on.
Babble on.
By the rivers of Babylon
I sat me down and wept.

A tear is a prism.
Did you know that?
Cry me a rainbow.

Do you see?
This is me—
a crazy old man
who no longer cares for numbers
or the moon
or the swinging planets
making their useless way
among indifferent stars.

Or is it I
who am useless?
Silent, or weeping
my tears the raindrops of Hades
my eyes the sodden windows
looking out on nighttime
or morning
or the soul
or nothing.

INTELLIGENT DESIGN

Who would dare
call this accident?
The pull of two bodies
is the inverse of the square
of the distance between them.
All bodies.
All the time.

The tiny birds return
on the same day each spring
and the Cam flows with ducklings
just in time for them to grow
and next season
to marshal ducklings of their own.

Who dares call it accident
that I can chart the shadow
of Trinity's tower
and know the season and the hour
now
and tomorrow
and yesterday
if I care to count backwards?

Who can think it accident
that the myriad stars are tame?
That they shine
in the same quadrant of the sky
tonight
and a hundred years ago
and a thousand?

I am a man of science
dedicated to the perfect truth
of all that I can measure.
Knight of numbers.
King of calculation. Calculus.

But even I own
that miracles are beyond measuring
that awe
is the wise man's response
to the work of the hand that formed us
and the eye that judged
and the mind
that figured all this out
and rendered it perfect.

Like the perfect equations
that I would write.
If only I could.

DR. NEWTON—A SHORT PANTOUM

When sick, I doctor myself,
Let no other nurse or dose me,
Keep my potions on a secret shelf
And guard my humours closely.

Let no other nurse or dose me,
None lend a helping hand
And guard my humours closely,
Cull herbs from sea and land.

None lend a helping hand.
I suffer no one near me,
Cull herbs from sea and land—
My compotes greatly cheer me.

I suffer no one near me.
No man can know my pain.
My compotes greatly cheer me.
Physician I remain.

Keep my potions on a secret shelf.
When sick, I doctor myself.

A TIME WILL COME

A time will come
when men—and even dames
will know these things:
how light becomes a wave
and creases the ether,
how sound
creases the ether
and bends the ear
toward meaning.

A time will come
when we know
exactly how a boy
becomes the image
of his father—
why one girl is lovely
but her sister is stout and dark.

A time will come
when we honour the fox
and chase the pox
before it chases us.
When the blind shall see
and the deaf shall hear
and few
to our sorrow
will credit
the Kingdom of God.

A time will come
when men—and even dames
will speak clearly across the void
will see magic images
beyond the art of alchemy.

A time will come
when the white, elusive stars
will speak their arcane names
and we will listen and learn
whether they are really there.

A time will come
when men—and even dames
will fly
when night will glow like day
when a hundred years
will sit upon the shoulders of a man
the way a decade sits there now.

A time will come
when all I've questioned
will be answered
and all I've pondered
will be proved.

A time will come
when I am nothing but a name—
a name that people whisper
when they realize
that all I wondered
learned and proved
is less than they know now.

MINE ENEMIES

I.

First came the man
who refused to be stepfather,
who cast me aside,
stole my mother
then gave her back to me
sick and old.

II.

Then there was Hooke.
A Godly man does not hate another.
So I don't use the word.

Hooke had a big mouth
and the big way
of the congenitally uncouth,
embracing the life of the city
like another man embraces a whore,
hanging around the coffeehouses
exhausting everyone
with his tiresome hypotheses
which he insisted were theories
because he couldn't tell the difference
between wishful thinking and proof.

Arguing with Hooke
was like taking sup with the Devil.
He turned me into a demon
who would prefer an hour in hell
to one more minute
engaged with his stupidity.

One day the bastard died
and freed me to become
what he had been:
President of the Royal Society,
its august ranks finally made
companionable
by the extraction of himself.

III.

Flamsteed, Astronomer Royal
lover of stars—who isn't?
Beloved of Charles II
who built the conservatory at Greenwich
for him
but left it vacant
a whited sepulcher
a great palace of emptiness.

No problem for Flamsteed.
He filled it himself
with lackies
with tools
and instruments
and implements
to enable his covert observations.

He meant to map the heavens
and keep its secrets to himself.

But I was leader.
I was master
of the Royal Society.
I forced him to make public
his imperfect work
or else I would shame him
before his monarch—
and his peers.

I lived to see him burn
every volume of his
faulty findings.

He claimed that by demanding
his work merely to aid my own
I'd ruined him.

I hope I did.

THE SHOULDERS OF GIANTS

"If I have seen further it is by standing on the shoulders of giants." Isaac Newton 1676, quoting Bernard of Chartres c. 1159

Humility is of no use
to a man who would wrestle
with creation.
So I looked to those
who in their boldness
emboldened me.

To stand on the shoulders of a giant
is to see
behind and before
to know what has been proven
and needs never be touched again.
To know what remains to be done
and can only be done by you.

To stand on the shoulders of a giant
is to view the landscape with the hawk's eye
to see from great height
the course of the river of knowing.

To stand on the shoulders of a giant
is to be a giant oneself.

THE BOY ON THE BEACH

"I seem to have been only like a boy playing on the
seashore, and diverting myself in now and then finding a
smoother pebble or a prettier shell than ordinary whilst
the great ocean of truth lay all undiscovered before me."
                                        Isaac Newton

The great ocean, the sea
eternity of approaching, receding waters
always new, always the same
connecting me who stands on the shore
to the far horizon
to the world invisible
beyond the line of the sky.

Great ocean, the sea
housing leviathan, minnow
and sidewise sliding creatures
who slither to and away
from the deep
seeking their crenelated scaly companions
or fleeing their hungry foes.

Great ocean of earth:
forests and fields,
cities, cathedrals of commerce
or of faith
the business of pauper and priest

the business of love
and those who would
fall prey to it.

Great ocean of the sky:
planets, stars, the moon
that comes and goes
and hides behind
the shoulder of the sun.

Great ocean of men:
heroes and reprobates
those who cherish joy
and those who harvest hate.
Children
aiming toward their fated life.
Women and men in their prime
making the world work—factory, mill.
The old, relics of themselves.

Great ocean of truth
that lay all about me,
so vast even thought
couldn't reach the edge of it.
Stars so far away
that a million years
was but the single step
of a man moving toward them.

The great ocean of truth
lay all about me.
I picked up a pebble
and studied its sea-worn smooth skin
and suddenly, I could see beneath--
atoms cavorting in a tiny void
and within each atom
smaller atoms
and on and on *ad infinitum*.

I stood on the shore of the ocean of truth
and I saw creation breathe
filling its infinite lungs
collapsing to the infinitesimal.

And I stand here
a boy with a pebble in his hand.

Shall I drop it to the sand
and leave it for
another wanderer to pick up?
Or should I cast it back
from whence it came
from whence I came
to whence I and the great sea
are ever longing to return?

E=mc2

"The changing of Bodies into Light, and Light into Bodies, is very conformable to the Course of Nature, which seems delighted with Transmutations."

Isaac Newton *Optiks*

I am light.
I am the rainbow
that slits through
the black board
nailed to my window.

I am light
a boy at play
in the sunfields
where heat greens
the sheep feed
and turns their supper
into the blankets that warm us.

I am a candle
in the silence of Trinity
a nightlight
by the bed
that is almost always
empty.

I am light
in the eyes of the confounded
the curious
the hungry for proof
and once
only once
in the gaze of a lover.

I am light
brother of the sweet, sweeping galaxies
of the shy moon
of the sky-reflecting waves
of the wind
that variegates the leaves.

I am light
a spark from the first
fire of Creation
an illumination
that shall endure.

AVE ATQUE VALE

I have spoken
and will say
no more.

"Nature was to him an open book, whose letters he could read without effort. The conceptions he used to reduce the material of experience to order seemed to flow spontaneously from experience itself, from the beautiful experiments which he ranged in order like playthings and described with an affectionate wealth of detail. In one person, he combined the experimenter, the theorist, the mechanic and, not least, the artist in exposition. He stands before us strong, certain, and alone; his joy in creation and his minute precision are evident in every word and every figure."

Albert Einstein on Isaac Newton

Rosemary Aubert has achieved world-wide attention with her Ellis Portal series. She is a Toronto writer, teacher, speaker and criminologist who mentors fresh mystery writers and treasures classic ones.

STRONG, CERTAIN AND ALONE

27717600R00059

Made in the USA
Columbia, SC
05 October 2018